*We are one in the Lord.
Love
Faith Johnson*

Inspirations By Faith

Poems

Faith Johnson

Copyright © 2007 by Faith Johnson

Inspirations By Faith
by Faith Johnson

Printed in the United States of America

Library of Congress Number: Txul-326-358

ISBN 978-1-60266-162-2

All rights reserved solely by the author. The author guarantees all contents are original and do not infringe upon the legal rights of any other person or work. No part of this book may be reproduced in any form without the permission of the author. The views expressed in this book are not necessarily those of the publisher.

Unless otherwise indicated, Bible quotations are taken from the King James Version. Copyright © 1928, 1956 by The John C. Winston Company. Copyright © 1964, 1972 by Zondervan Publishing House.

www.xulonpress.com

From the heart of Faith, have come forth reservoirs of inspirational wealth to share with those that may read the pages that follow. I am betrothed to the written word of God; it is the lamp unto all paths of life and the voyage to creative thought.

For the gracious anchorage of my family and The Church of Our Redeemer, these writings are in veneration for these my people of faith.

Faith Johnson

Contents

Healing of the Soul

Another Chance	11
Forgiveness Has No Charge	12
Forgiveness Brings Power	13
The Prodigal	14
Who Are You	15
Ashes To Pearls	16
Vessel	17
As I think About It	18
Thinking It Over	19
Renew My Dream	20
The Darkest Tear	21
Set Me Free	22
A Comforting Song	24
I Will Proclaim	25
Cherish Others	26
A Challenge Of the Faith	27
Life To Death	28
Breakout	29
Strength	30
Awaken The Dream	31
Lifestyles	32
You Haven't Heard Me In a While	33
Jairus's Daughter	34
Little Vessel	35
Forgivers	36
The Boy	37
Upon The Altar	39

The Victory

An Awesome Birth 41
I thought I Knew 42
Opportunity 43
In the Sanctuary 44
No Matter What 46
The Highest Place 48
I Shall Not Thirst Again 49
Promises 50
The Soldier 52
AnotherYear 53
LiftOff 54
Creation 55

Lonely Times

Loneliness 56
Draw A Picture 57
He Is With Us 58
Take Root 59
Affliction 60
Struggling 61
Wondering 62
Alienation 63
Rising Above The Storm 65
Teen-Age Cry 67

Encouragement

The Miracle Of Change 69
A Chance In Time 70
I Am Fulfilled 71
Life Goes On 72
New Life 73

I Will Stand	75
The Secret Intruder	76
Encouragement	77
Always There	78
The Village Green	79
You Are	80
Honorable Father	81
Forever	82
Strengthened	83
The Mask	84

The Master's Hand

How Vibrant Are We	86
The Work Is Done	87
Treasures	88
Today	89
Power In His Hand	90
Angelic Breeze	91
Ring Every Bell And Chime	92
Oh Holy Spirit	93
Everlasting Father	94
Priceless Love	95
Sacrifice	96
Salvation	97
Approaching Him	98
Victorious	99
Dayspring	100
Ministering	101
Prayer	102

Tranquility

Peace	104
Words	105

A Baby's Prayer 106
In The Glimpse Of The Day 107
A Father's Hymn 108
In The Joy Of Life 109
Reaching 110
Burst Forth 111
This Morning 112
Freedom 113
Quiet Spirit 114
The Night 116

The Ways Of Love

Clay 117
It's Me 118
Cry Aloud 119
Grandparents 120
A Love That Satisfies 121
Building 122
Blessings 123
Endless Love 124
These Two As One 125
Mothers Of Honor 126
The Light Of Night 128

Another Chance

No one knew what I had done
For I was called the chosen one.

I'm no different from the rest
I just happen to fail the test.

Cravings in me caused the sin
My inner will had worn so thin.

I can't believe I made a slip
I thought I had a solid grip.

There is no secret place to hide
And what about my family's pride.

Lord you came and found me there
Walking the road called nowhere.

You helped me at my weakest point
Forgive my spirit through every joint.

Thank you Lord for removing my sin
Please let me start over again.

Forgiveness Has no Charge

Thought no one knew the secret
Yet self could barely keep it
It was written upon the face
This thing some called disgrace.

Just wanting to run and hide
Yet thoughts of human pride
What would the people think?
Hidden fantasies began to sink.

The courage to face it all
Twas written on every wall
Who was lurking near?
Someone take away the fear.

The thought of revealed things
Might clip the herald wings
Oh let it all come out
A voice began to shout

Destroy the painful song
God came to free the wrong
Oh weary heart dislodge
Forgiveness has no charge.

Forgiveness Brings Power

Forgiveness is the divine spiritual plan
The Father sent by the Paschal Lamb
The freedom to give to those that offend
That Jesus the savior might enter in.

Would you hold back and take the blame?
Give power to rescue from sin and shame
Refuse to forgive the mistakes of souls
That you may take a hand in control.

Do not create a heart of grim
You cannot hold a place with Him
Your life should reflect inner joy
That the enemy cannot taunt or destroy.

Will you carry the burden He took away?
When you kneel to pray what will you say?
Forgiveness always gives way to victory
A standard of pride that all will see.

Forgiveness is given to those that bruise
Even when feeling utterly misused
Give up the selfish will to not forgive
Let Christ the Savior forever heal.

The Prodigal

Oh prodigal please come home
Your place is not to roam
The table is always set
All is paid; there is no debt.

You may have lost your way
Your thoughts are in disarray
It does not matter where you've been
Just let the Savior abide within

Don't look at others to judge your life
For they too once waged through strife
Do you accept the call to come?
Praise God for whom all blessings are from.

Yes this prodigal will be found
Life has worn me to the ground
I'm thankful for discipleship
It raised me from this shameful slip.

Oh come again sweet Savior dear
Let your presence be forever near
All your riches await me now
I live today, you showed me how!

Who Are You

What are you trying to do?
Is it all some strange taboo?
This mask that you wear
Is it strictly utter despair?

Put away this whole façade
Don't you really find it odd?
Being something that you're not
So distorted in your thought.

You're really not the blame
It's the fire and the flame
Will you isolate your goal?
Change the future that you hold?

You walk on broken glass
Living out the painful past
When will you break it down?
Your life is so profound.

You have the tools for power
Change your life this very hour
Just look within yourself
You have God given wealth.

Ashes to Pearls

The skin was broken, a trickle down
Scarlet and crimson spilled to the ground
No voice would come to ever speak
To free a call so utterly dim and weak.

Who would conceive such an atrocious deed?
Moving to bombard a mournful stampede
Hoping the harsh trauma would soon depart
Where was the sweet lifestyle needed to start?

A crushing of the flowered intimate peace
Lying beneath the spotted sheets
Innocent voice would ever proclaim
Revealing an image of the invading shame.

Where was the holster and guarding guide?
Helping to maintain the human pride
Hiding heartaches can become a skill
It may seem improper to let it spill

Rise up from the ashes and be a pearl
Walk laced in pride created boy or girl
Cuts and bruises take time to heal
Let dignity rise to its highest reel.

Vessel

I went before the Lord in prayer
This burden alone I could not bear
The magnitude of this great ordeal
Seemed more than I cared to conceal.

I talked with others around my home
They kept leading me back to the throne
It seems so easy to share how one feels
Even though I transcend to higher hills.

In anguish I said, oh poor pitiful me
I thought I carried the safeguard key
Is an open heart the way to down?
Or is this the way to build a crown.

Bewildered I felt alone at first
I took faith and broke the curse
I heard the voice of my inner being
Please come my child under my wing.

In wisdom, the outcome He foreknew
Determination is now my positive view
When life seemed so out of shape
I was the vessel God would make.

As I Think About It

As I think about life
And how to avoid strife
A picture of peaceful things
Does not seem to be extreme.

As I think about sin
It brings damnation to all men
An alternate plan has been derived
A blood sacrifice, He did provide.

As I think about this sacrifice
I must provide some advice
A hand, a heart, a way to turn
Is all a soul might actually yearn.

As I think of bewildered souls
Drifting along with little goals
I must seek to be a greater light
To those that suffer thru the night.

As I think about my words in speech
May it always be a language in reach
Healing, instructing, building the man
Ministering has become an integral plan.

Thinking It Over

Shall we really listen to mind our place?
Swallow our pride and suffer disgrace
Walk as shadows at dusk and dawn
Dare to congregate on the front lawn.

Dispense thoughts in measures of small
Behind the prism of a barricade wall
Dare to mix, create, or properly speak
Work only with continual defeat.

Live as neighbors of worldwide slum
To mix the cakes measured with rum
Coming by day, leaving late by night
Unfair labors and human rights.

To wear a suit or conservative dress
Would make one different from the rest
Misplaced beneath the office mat
The mystery of the applicant's contract.

The day is not over in the rise of time
Stand to your feet, challenge the prime
Walk among men undefeated in class
Mounted by dignity, in victory surpass.

Renew My Dream

Needles in my fingers, where do I turn?
Walking in the fast lane, will I ever learn?
My head became so heavy, I could not win
Good times became bad judgment in the end.

Thinking I had the tools, for my weary soul
Using new worldly tactics, yet they are of old
Building roads of terror, despite of disbelief
There was no satisfaction or any inward peace.

Gambling at a dream only for temporary pay
My heart kept hoping for a better day
Wrestling with a vision, veiled without hope
Thoughts to make it big to just impress folk.

I know I should be living by the Master's plan
It seems so slow in coming to reach my hand
Now pondering for forgiveness, I am to blame
I was seeking for a dream for mere selfish gain.

The Darkest Tear

The darkest tear
Becomes a human fear
A silent night
Births strength and might.

A yearning soul
Fulfills the goal
A jubilant stand
Walks by demand.

A forward step
Is a promise kept
Enslaving dreams
So real it seems.

The desert place
Makes a glowing face
Bridge despair
With gentle care.

A fearless quest
Results in rest
Beyond the grave
There is no slave.

Set Me Free

Going through life's daily test
Trying hard to do my best
Why are things so very tough?
Release me from these handcuffs.

Life is pounding in my ears
Daily trying to bring forth cheer
Sometimes things aren't going right
I don't want to live in strife!

Lord will you possibly hear from me?
I know you really set me free
Always disclosing my thoughts to you
In years past you brought me through.

Rid me of yesterday's fault
Let it all come to a halt
Disrupt the memory from the slate
I really am carrying all I can take.

Knowing its not too very late
To turn around and close the gate
Assured there are other open doors
To walk forth on greater shores.

Turning on a new light switch
May cause my life to be enriched
Just taking on a new direction
Will surely impact a bright reflection.

You have been my sheltering tower
Thank you for magnificent power
Starting a new fragrant day
Lord will you pave the way?

A Comforting Song

On misty skies
Or sun filled days
Angels follow close.

In brave affairs
Or fallen dreams
Angels guide with care.

When devastation
Brings humiliation
Angels touch the brow.

On broken ground
Or stepping stones
Angels bring victory.

Sleepless nights
Through restlessness
Angels kneel in prayer.

In loving words
Or kindness serve
Angels speak through you!

I Will Proclaim

Proclaim your destiny, proclaim your year
Tell God's people to not have fear
Victory will come within your reach
It's not about eloquent speech

The word declares the proclamation
Open your hearts in humble affirmation
Receive by faith His Goodyear plan
All it takes is your spoken command.

Do not sit under the shady trees
Blessings come from bending knees
Lazy worth thrown far in the past
Sharp minds is what you must cast.

Words and action are terrific measures
This is what will bring you treasures
Paying your bills and dare to borrow
Will be your triumph on tomorrow.

Gamblers use up God's resources
To carry out their wicked forces
Live for Jesus a life that's grand
Upon his principles surely stand.

A soaring spirit will lift the head
A tired spirit just lies in bed
Negative thoughts have no aim
Proclaim your blessings it's more gain.

Cherish Others

I will smile and laugh with those I meet
As I walk along the street
Keeping in mind souls to win
To share creation that never ends.

The bliss to see the good in others
Moments of love with sisters and brothers
Tasteful compliments in a genuine tone
Being realistic do not groan.

Then walk upon the sands of life
Hoping to share the name of Christ
It is a place I love to roam
It comes close from the heart of home.

Favors are tasks shared with friends
Never forget how good it's been
Do not ask or think it back
For different waters will fill your pack.

Give the love the world should hold
Taking candles burning bold
Give a wick to light the way
As you move throughout the day.

Cherish all the good God brings
As it comes in helping things
Make the good spring from the bad
Cause a soul to be made glad.

A Challenge of The Faith

I'm Daddy's little girl and boy
Delighting in the sound
As I walk in this world
Shall I be renowned?

I'm mother's generation
A reflection in her mirror
Her morning meditation
A destiny becoming clearer.

Protect me from myself
Oh spirit guide me there
Dear God my mental health
My everlasting fare.

Instill in me the pride
To know the right and wrong
Not only to survive
Thus rise with my song.

Upon my family's wings
A heritage of their grace
Deliverance breaks to bring
A challenge of the faith.

Life to Death

You passed from life to death
No matter what the quest
An outcome all must face
Regardless of the race.

Memories of the past
Yet in the heart to last
Sorrow, grief, and pain
A measure of disdain.

Thoughts of you today
Wishing you had stayed
Awakened from a dream
So real it certainly seems.

Remembering all your words
As if they've just been heard
Loving you now and then
For it shall never end.

Your special favored manner
Written on every banner
Forever in the clouds
Your memory leaves us proud.

Breakout

Your prison has no bars
There are no isolated rooms
The iron chains are not there
What are your barriers?

There are no guardsmen there
The gates are not visible
Yet you are locked in
In the prison of your mind.

Your thoughts are narrow
Your vision is impaired
Do you dream of a break out?
It is time for a breakthrough.

Remove the weakness
Put on strength
Forgive the offender
Forget the intruder.

The bondage is broken
You are set free
Walk in the water
You are born again.

Strength

There is a grand premiere
That takes away the fear
In the fellowship of the soul
Tender moments will unfold.

Just bury sullen thoughts
Temptation boldly brought
Tame the bitter growth
Situations that provoke.

Walk on higher hills
Focus on greater skills
Forget the hurtful past
Let forgiveness ever last.

Discipline is the boast
Instruction takes an oath
Fundamental is the task
Build only what will last.

Maintain a pleasant view
Refreshing as the dew
Plant a healthy seed
Strength is the perfect deed.

Awaken the Dream

Who can change a written plan?
A willing vessel, an open hand
Reaching forth to grasp the bar
To lift above what seems so far.

To make a difference, to take a stand
Create a vision within the land
Awake a dream; think it through
Pray for wisdom, when there's no clue.

Dispense the grain that has been kept
This is the beginning; just take the step
Refresh the spirit; let it flow
There is a seed just watch it grow.

Muzzle not to think the thought
Release the task that's really sought
Burn the past; yes, build the bridge
Walk every hill and rocky ridge.

Where is the pompous perfect one?
Who said, " Oh it couldn't be done"
Work defeats an idle dream
What is sown shall be redeemed.

Lifestyles

Do not avoid the question
Why is there deception?
Whispering in the night
Everything seems all right.

Looking in the mirror
Vision not any clearer
Washed by life's hoses
Tossing the wilted roses.

Don't try to live a lie
Just give it one more try
Learn facts that are true
It's all up to you.

Climb the heavenly wall
Faith won't let you fall
Stay prayerful as you talk
Prepare your daily walk.

You Haven't Heard Me in a While

Good morning Lord this is your child
I know you haven't heard me in a while
Things were going so awesomely good
All my trials, I have faithfully stood.

Despite being tremendously clad
I knew I needed to talk with you Dad
Last night I did not rest very well
That unction means to rise and compel.

I'm sorry to neglect my time with you
The pressures of life nudged me through
Lord I kneel in prayer this hour
Bathe me in your mercy filled shower.

With every breath and tender touch
I realize Lord you love me so much
Spark my soul in dutiful devotion
Fill my spirit with prayerful emotion.

I praise you for who I am
You guided me as your precious lamb
My heart is thankful for all you do
Remind me daily to pray to you.

Jairus's Daughter

Child wrapped in the Ruler's word
Come forth now and be heard
Arise from what seems dead
Pull the cloth from thy head.

Hear the call from the land
The thundering clap of hands
Awake from thy sleep
Escape the darkness of the deep.

Open thine tightened eyes
The Almighty God speaks wise
"Talitha Cuma"
Let life consume her!!!

The Master of living waters
Called forth Jairus's daughter
Tell no one what is done
This is the fulfillment of the Son.

Little Vessel

The little vessel came to a place
With heaven's light upon her face
Pure untarnished by the world
Innocently groomed, a cultured pearl.

Read from the master's script, then shaped
Delicately mannered, poised and draped
Followed the leading of life's manual guide
Filled every room with sweet feminine pride.

Princess of the castle, she is crowned
Her laughter embraced all those around
She grew in statue, fair wise and tall
Surrounded by angels, listening for the call.

The vessel was given away in love
Sent with protection from above
Scarred, then broken and not repaired
Seemed as though no one cared.

The Master Potter came before long
Bound up the pieces, forgave the wrong
Pronounced a stronger vessel still
Walking according to the Master's will.

Forgivers

They hurt
Yet not for long
They build
Thus stand strong.

They cry
Yet never drown
When doors are closed
New ones are found.

Broken hearted
Yet they repair
When there is pain
They provide the care.

They are not the crowd
Yet always seen
They bare the cause
Try to redeem.

When frowned upon
They share the good
They hold to wisdom
Promote brotherhood

They recover peace
In thundering storms
When pushed aside
Forgivers reform.

The Boy

Behind the prison wall
The incident seem so small
Paying for all the wrong
A place where criminals belong.

The years were passing by
He asked himself why?
So sorry for the pain
What did he have to gain?

Being led by the crowd
Their voices soared so loud
He tossed his dream away
His mood began to sway.

Too late for second thoughts
His mind was so distraught
He must tame his angry soul
Pray for mercy to unfold.

The cry of being free
Dear God please rescue me
Forgiveness became a part
The boy had a repenting heart.

Walking on his own
Thank God for a Christian home
Released from prison strife
I will not look back twice!

Now that I am a man
I hold the Bible in my hand
I tell the message of Christ
How He changed my life.

Upon The Altar

My gifts have been stifled
Oh help me Lord on high
My hands have been tied
Yet I pray without ceasing
There is no alibi.

In the sanctuary my voice is not heard
I call upon your name in silence
My body is upon the altar
I give of myself to thee
I rest in your presence.

I run in the city
They don't know me there
Yet I am familiar to all
I have worked among the people
Their eyes acknowledge my efforts.

I find a reservoir
It becomes the sanctity of my soul
I bathe in the mist of life
My thoughts are renewed
I am resurrected.

I have found myself
The horizon is an inspiration
The birds cheer me on
The winds blow on my countenance
The trees mark the stability of my worth.

I focus on all creative things
I am silent, yet I speak
I cry, yet I am overcome with laughter
I am of few words
Yet, I am the volume among men.

An Awesome Birth

The awesome birth
To save the church
Jesus the Christ
Born to give life

So glad He came
To rebuke the shame
None can deny
Just glorify!

All praise this day
His merciful way
All heaven rejoice
Make Him your choice

Light the candle
Upon every mantle
An awesome birth
Confirm its worth!

I Thought I Knew

I thought I knew the perfect way
Became self reliant every day
I held my head level high
Winked to others passing by.

Schemed and planned no one knew
Came to worship among who's who
Smiled yet barely showed my grief
Just the place to seek relief.

All at once my heart bells rang
As my head began to hang
No one knew my hidden fears
Until my eyes burst forth with tears.

I sat not knowing what to do
The spoken word cut me through
In spite of all my self-righteous gain
Clouds poured down ministering rain.

My troubles became a dead end street
I fell upon the mercy seat
I thought I had maintained control
Until Jesus came and saved my soul.

Opportunity

To accept the challenge
To act by inspiration
To siege availability
This is opportunity.

The chance to develop
The impulse for performance
To step toward creativity
This is opportunity.

To reach for love
To forget the past
To start again
This is opportunity.

To be unique
To walk in worthiness
To live in victory
This is opportunity.

To live with passion
To discover treasures
To climb a mountain
This is opportunity.

To embrace the promise
To serve the Lord
To open the door
This is opportunity.

In The Sanctuary

I will come to the sanctuary
Lulled by the smoking incense
To the altar, I am compelled
I kneel in the presence of the Almighty.

My mind is induced by His glory
I am overwhelmed by His goodness
My head is touched with oil
The veil is upon my face.

My eyes are as a missioner
The lips of my mouth are sealed
I am beyond myself now
In the silence of the temple, I pray.

I look upon the mercy seat
The candles light the way
The scroll becomes my passage
It is the guide for the soul.

Shall I speak in the sanctuary?
Will I break the awesome silence?
My heart pumps repetitive lyrics
My voice parades the quiet place.

I chant praises to the song
I release my hidden fears
The gates seem to open
I have come too far to leave.

I stand in the sanctuary
Beholding the beauty here
This is the perfect dwelling place
Where my life has become an art.

No Matter What

No matter what the despair
There are people that care
No matter where you may go
Trust in what you already know.

When you are in the lion's den
Hoping it will come to an end
Take a look within your soul
Quietly let the future unfold.

Life is full of beautiful things
Focus on what it really means
Inhale for a moment, breathing deep
Think of what you really seek.

Awake your mind from any gloom
Let your focus slowly resume
Be creative let it flow
Sip your cup very slow.

Refresh and build your curious mind
Know that you are one of a kind
Release yourself to enjoy the best
Let all strife and tension rest.

What do you desperately want to learn?
What is it that you dare to yearn?
Trust the fibers of your thread
Bury things that are obviously dead.

No matter what you've recently found
Keep your feet on solid ground
Have a hope that's sound & pure
Thank God for a healthy cure.

The Highest Place

When faith shuts down
Angels hover around
To pray in your stead
Gently anoint your head.

When prayer brings its grace
You're in the highest place
Just let your faith release
Then favor will increase.

He is the one to seek
Say not that you're weak
Come enter into his rest
You're sure to pass the test.

Receive this perfect love
Descending as a dove
Build up your fallow ground
There is a cross and crown.

I Shall Not Thirst Again

Power moves within my life
It is my lowest point
Building strength within my soul
I thought to never own.

It is a friend that lives close by
A knowledge that is taught
Springing from the well of life
A feeling that makes me whole.

Erupt in me oh power source
As I breathe the test of time
Daring to overcome the least
The pain within my heart.

My body became a playground
Where I first learned to walk
Heal the broken places
As I rise from the falls.

Plant the seed in my mind
Give way to fruitful thought
A work that becomes a skill
Preparing to grow thereby.

Power is my drinking spout
A path I could not find
I climbed beyond the dryness
I shall not thirst again.

Promises

I will walk and not pretend
Inasmuch I face the end
Promising to forgive
In this life I now live.

No compromise for sin
The battle I want to win
Just to lead by example
A faith that is ample.

Walk with fulfilling worth
Spread the word on this earth
Making a sacrifice
I want to pay the price.

To live without regrets
The truth to select
Be proper in my speech
Many souls I hope to reach.

I'll love every child
Be gentle and mild
Fight for the right
Pray for guided sight.

Love my family with pride
An inheritance to provide
Maintain the righteous stalk
As I teach them how to walk.

Shall I sleep without fear?
When the Savior calls me near
My work is now done
I am called the chosen one.

The Soldier

As I stand upon this land
Framed by the Almighty
Sure of my position
My focus is upon Him.

I'm ushered into combat
My mission now is clear
Walking upon the battlefield
My fear is upon his shoulders.

My eyes behold His glory
As I march across the plain
The hills become my refuse
The valley my lingering post.

My heart holds the declaration
This path I chose to take
To stand upon this privilege
Commissioned to do His will.

Another Year

Another year, I'm blessed to see
Oh dear Savior I give praise to thee
I never thought I'd live this long
Through the years you made me strong.

At times I thought to turn around
My friends just beat me to the ground
The world has been a beautiful place
I found the courage to endure the race.

As leaves fall and then return
I get the benefits I have earned
The rain comes to soothe the earth
I have been given a firm rebirth.

Each day becomes an uphill climb
I take advantage of the precious time
Life is not just centered on me
I give fruit to others from my tree.

Each day I shall build on the plan
Knowing I have a foundation that stands
I will fill my well of water here
Thanking God for another year.

Lift Off

Never feel defeated
Even when cheated

Lift up your head
Fasten to the thread

Warm by the fire
Music to inspire

Find a way to smile
Through every trial

Aim for the best
An old familiar quest.

Creation

The forests are the trees
The body bends on knees
The seed yields the fruit
The ground holds the root.

Life is a mystery
Books hold history
Love flows to heart
To begin is to start.

Water makes a river
Shaking is a quiver
Fall tells the season
Intuition leads to reason

Speech develops praise
Weeks result from days
Peas line in the pod
Creation is of God.

Loneliness

Loneliness sat upon my chair
Whispered softly for no one was there
Moving close to tell in my ear
All is quiet what must I fear

A shadow comes to arrest my sight
As daylight moves out for the night
Who will knock upon my door?
To bring in food and do my chore.

All my folk are so busy now
Knowing a way is there some how
Limbs seem heavy, feet do tire
There is much I seem to desire.

Loneliness came and rocked me asleep
My head lay in the pillow deep
Rest released a peaceful smile
In Jesus arms, I am as a child.

Draw a Picture

Smile when heartbroken
Draw sunshine when the way is dim.

Put your hands and feet in action
Draw yourself running after a fall.

Swallow when all choked up
Draw a light shining in dark places.

Wear a life jacket amidst the storm
Draw yourself walking on the water.

Picture bright eyes when full of tears
Draw a rainbow, a covenant of faith.

He Is With Us

Give heed to the Highest Power
He is with us through every hour
He is not a million miles away
He hears every word we say.

He never makes a single mistake
He is there through all heartbreaks
When we wonder where to turn
It is our prayers He really yearns.

Sometimes when we fall behind
He is ever faithful and so kind
When we choose the wrong direction
He gathers us under His protection.

Let's live each day as our last
Leaving all the sinful past
We know not what the future holds
Each day His mercy to us unfolds.

He's given us another chance
So we praise Him with a dance
Commit your promise to ever stay
Know that He will provide the way!

Take Root

There is a thirsty place
Inside every human soul
It hides beneath the exterior
No one sees the planted seed.

There is a desert home
Between the marrow and the bone
It eats away at mind and spirit
Yet hoping to be free.

There is a quiet thought
That lives in loneliness
Sleeping among the thistles
Upon life's sandy ground.

Arise oh broken leaflets
Sprinkle mist upon your earth
Break through little sprouts
Take root and live again.

Affliction

When one gives others a chance
And the returns never come in
That is affliction

When one bears responsibility
And the burden gets heavier
That is affliction

When one declares the mountaintop
And cannot come out of the valley
That is affliction

When truth is your character
And deception shakes its hands
That is affliction

When one falls down
 And no one lends a hand
That is affliction

After sharing your substance
The meal barrel is empty
Expect a miracle, affliction has passed.

Struggling

I lost my spouse to sin
I cannot let the devil win
I pray at every waking day
Oh Lord give me what to say.

How may I change this fate?
Put love where there is hate
Where is the strength to live?
I only hope to forgive.

My spouse is wondering off
Moving from the tablecloth
There is no loving stare
Only the eyes of despair.

I struggle all alone
Where is the happy home?
The breaking of each day
Leads my spouse astray.

Committed to silent rest
I stand to do my best
I look beyond the stars
Oh Lord, please take charge.

Wondering

Longing to fit in
A hunger deep within
Laughing in the crowd
Standing very proud.

Engaging in small talk
Yet pulled from the stalk
Having a sense of direction
Acquainting little affection.

Feeling so alone
Wondering from the home
Wanting to escape
Decisions yet to make.

Desiring to reach forth
Afraid to make a choice
Holding on to life
Ever feeling strife.

Is this a common way?
Fainthearted on this day
Reframing from the wrong
Listening to a song.

Encouraged to take spirit
Reminded of the lyrics
Inspiration fills the heart
This is the place to start.

Alienation

A separation from the home of things
Togetherness lost on wounded wings
A nation that has lost its creed
Land without a trust or deed.

Blinded from night and day
A feeling of drifting away
The creature that has lost its brood
A performing art without prelude.

In love with the cold ill hearted
A vehicle that can never be started
A stranger among his native place
The sprinter that can make no haste.

Isolated by a loss of connection
Governing laws without protection
Deliberate attempts to pull one down
To be a queen without a crown.

To claim the victory and yet not win
Estrangement from a loving friend
A portrait that will not be mounted.
To live this life and not be counted.

A distorted view when the way is clear
The peaceful moment laced with fear
To sin and not feel forgiven
To starve when there is ample provision.

To have authority yet no power
To move in time and miss the hour
The work of the house on sinking sand
To never be guided by the Master's hand.

Rising Above The Storm

She did not say a word
No clue that she ever heard
The words that were spoken here
As she sat by the river near.

The waves were rippling in
Tears locking under her chin
Her knees embracing her hands
The feet mangled in the sand.

Boats with wind blown sails
The sound of creatures in detail
She uttered an exhausting sigh
Wiped her eyes partly dry.

Remembering things of the past
Memories that seem to last
A thought became the dream
What did it really mean?

Would she rise above the storm?
Could she possibly see reform?
The weary of this quest
Brought thoughts insisting, yes.

He spoke clearly in the quake
I will never leave nor forsake
It was hard to forgive herself
Yet she discovered a sea of wealth.

As she walked upon the shore
Her spirit began to soar
She heard the words within
I have wiped away the sin.

Teen-age Cry

Beneath the ivory tower
It is where I live
This is my real house
All dressed up in Me.

I'm only young once
So give me a break
I will learn some day
What is life about anyway?

There are so many choices
Sometimes I'm overwhelmed
How hard is life?
Who made it this way?

Why can't I be left alone?
I think I can help myself!
My head seems to lead
Yet my heart is flashing red.

Perhaps I should listen
My mouth is quiet now
Whisper in my ear
Preach your lesson plans.

Speak from your tower
I want to hear your call
Where are you?
Where am I going?

I need another chance
I'll walk as I am told
Someone let me out!
I'm afraid, is it too late?

The Miracle of Change

My life has turned around
Twas a miracle I was found!
Entangled in all the danger
Love treated me as a stranger.

God has a glow upon my face
Living in honor and not disgrace.
I had walked on tear stained floors
Lived with bars and armored doors.

No more yelling through the night
Promiscuity put out of sight
Discarded the old profane
Took the road to ultimate change.

Privileged to have a friend
A hope for a prosperous end
What is this thing called fate?
Thank God it's not too late

A Chance in Time

A second chance bear me please
Upon the waters a gentle breeze
Tossed and torn on splinted wings
The surfeit of a thousand things

Rushing through grains of sand
Oh dear God the failing man
A ship will come to bring the news
Amidst the row of standing pews

The silence of the dreadful night
A pulse of life now in flight
Return again and lead me through
The promise kept, a vow to renew.

Running toward a chance in time
To begin again, now is mine
Believing is as the ocean wave
Rushing upon the noble and brave!

I Am Fulfilled

Twas in the gentle breeze, I felt His presence
It was the calmness of the night, I felt at peace
The leaves seem to kindly whisper of his greatness
In the silence I beheld Him!

As I walked along the stone called cobble,
On this solid foundation, I shall stand and not fall.
I shall walk and be confident, for I am steadfast
I am in Him a rock!

The flowing fountain along the way,
Reminded me of the outpour of His spirit
Overflowing in the ecstasy of propitious joy
I am fulfilled!

Surrounded by the greenery of His creation
I absorb life in abundance
I am consumed by His goodness
I am challenged!

I look beyond the circumstance compassed about me
I am ushered out of the door of perplexity
I lock the gate to all unhappiness
I shall not return!

Life Goes On

No matter what has happened
Life goes on
When patience rules and pity ends
Renew the spirit and start again.

Errors are just stepping-stones
That pave the path to the road ahead
Through every faulty situation
The Lord became the propitiation.

Remember pain is not forever
It does take time to heal
Just lean on the Savior
He exalts with His great favor.

Misfortunes may cause setbacks
Yet operate with success
Take stamina, will and power
He will help every hour.

Don't give up on the self
Rebuild and be steadfast
Let persistence be the goal
Opportunities will unfold.

New Life

The Lord gave me seed
It is now conceived
There is life inside
It has given me new pride

The mystery of it all
The blessing of the call
One has become two
Learning what to do.

Nervous and afraid
Decisions to be made
Thinking of a name
Enthusiastic aim.

The time is finally here
To birth a life so dear
Heavy in travail
The babe shall prevail!

A new life is born
Humanity blow the horn
Behold the mother now
So humble does she bow.

Lord I give my child to you
The perfect plan to pursue
The child is taught in faith
Mother praying for God's grace.

A mother does her best
Then God does the rest
To teach by the word
Each prayer will be heard.

I Will Stand

I will stand and speak the word
For I know I will be heard
I will stand and walk this path
Even if others sit and laugh.

I will extend my hands in praise
Despite the gloom filled day
I will move beyond my fears
Today I will wipe away the tears.

I will lift the heavy curtain
Move forward that's for certain
I will have an aim in view
For my God is faithful and true

My mind has taken the task
To forget the things of the past
I traded my ashes for beauty
Self-allegiance is active in duty.

I will stand and drink from the urn
My life has taken a turn
I will run in the light of day
Hurdle over obstacles set in clay

I will stand and sing my song
The stanzas poised not too long
I will march to the rhythm beat
I've triumphed over defeat.

The Secret Intruder

There has come to all a secret birth
That simmers cunningly at your worth
An intruder of your most secret place
That finds its way through an open space.

When love should ignite your entrance door
Obstruction enters with a subtle war
There is no knock or alarming sound
Only an attempt to bear the spirit down.

Following close pushing every cue lever
Attempting to be shrewd and very clever
To tiptoe in and secure the highest seat
About the time for your evening peak.

Dare not to be challenged or bent in despair
Muzzle the thought, be bold and aware
Situations may come that are hard to digest
Evict the intrusion and flee for success.

Encouragement

The beauty of a quiet moment
To sit and think of Him
Pulling of unpleasantness
I hold abreast my peace.

I ponder past and present dreams
I thought not to behold
It seemed a long way off
Yet time has brought it near.

In the silence of the night
My heart can only speak
The gifts within my soul
Unfold to heights unknown.

The strength of life I live
Shall neither crush nor bruise
I hold to my foundation
Encouraged by my hope.

Always There

I stand in your weakness
Behind in gentle meekness
I long to build you up
Provide your daily cup.

I walk and feel your pain
When you seem to have no aim
You may not see me there
When filled with utter despair.

I'm in your secret closet
When thinking you have lost it
I'm in every open door
When your spirit seems to soar.

I'm in every bending knee
I've come to make you free
I'm in every rise and fall
Just listening for your call.

I live within your soul
To cleanse and make you whole
I see your stream of tears
I protect you through your fears

I carry you to the mountain
To drink the refreshing fountain
I speak to give correction
I am divine direction.

The Village Green

I'm guilty of this most honest deed
For my Lord put the truth in seed
I will not come to serenade your mind
Nor move you to heights sublime.

I'll lead you to the Village Green
Fill your heart with life's harvest beam
This you do for those folks you meet
Remove their shoes and wash their feet.

Share a verse of the word in truth
Careful not to sound aloof
Ask if there is trouble or fear
Tell everyone that Jesus is forever near.

Feed a soul with the fruit of love
Let a sweet-spirit ascend like a dove
Deeds must come from home at first
For this shows the power of your worth.

Giving love is a much-needed task
For you rescue those that may never ask
So, a sincere thought is often seen
As carrying the world under your wing.

You Are

You are incredible
Allow your gifts to work.

You are benevolent
Give to the unfortunate.

You are a servant
Put forth your hands to help.

You are strength
Gather the weak.

You have salvation
Spread the gospel story

You are exalted
Remain humble.

Honorable Father

You are the heart of the earth
You are sculptured with worth
As you tread upon the land
Cultivating seed with a gentle hand.

Thorns and thistles bruised your feet
Yet you remained humble and discreet
You have risen from the fall
To father is an awesome call.

Your WELL sometimes have been dry
Yet you primed the when and the why
As father you take the time
To realize you're not divine.

You walk as a ministering priest
As your power is gently released
You train children's mind
You would never be unkind.

As father you lead by example
Your bread is the perfect sample
Guarding those that wonder away
In hard trials you teach them to pray.

You kneel to bless your wife
You maintain a harmonious life
As father you've done your best
You are the patriot of success.

Forever

Forever is an eternity
Bearing a burden seems forever
Yet today brings a new beginning.

Forever was just yesterday
I lived happy in the moment
Forever was not a focus.

The hours of pain was forever
Then the pain became silent
Forever was lost in the night.

My spirit is free
I know it is not forever
It is for now and tomorrow.

My hope is forever
It is as the flowing waters
My faith is the present seed.

Forever is projection
Eternity is a passage way
Now paves the future.

I laugh for a time
Cry when unhappy
It is the sanctity of the soul.

My prayers are forever
My struggle is just for today
I look for eternity, forever.

Strengthened

Minister to the soul
The essence of being whole
Why bother to explain
Any past that brings shame.

Sharing all the best
Boldness fulfills the test
Climb to the highest peak
Elevated from defeat.

Ministering lifts one up
So drink of its gentle cup
Now lift the yielded hands
An applause that understands.

Strengthen any weakness
Take on the gift of meekness
Celebrate yourself
It offers worthy wealth.

Let your spirit flow
Plant seeds that will grow
Ministering will permeate
Graciously alter mistakes.

Builders look to the cross
Vicariously save the lost
Each day is an open door
To walk and expect more.

The Mask

You wear a silly mask
There are things you just can't grasp
Hiding from yourself
Keeps you in declining health.

Your life has become so blind
You resent those that are kind
Regardless of the demand
Please try to take a stand.

It's not from where you've come
It's your accumulated sum
It's not really where you've been
Be the master of thoughts within.

Release the bitter grip
Send maliciousness on a trip
Conquer your spiritual worth
Pull off the masking curse.

Rise and start again
Put the past in the wind
Gather the things that are good
Create a pleasant neighborhood.

Build your philosophy on hope
Forget the downward slope
Think on powerful things
It 's not as dreary as it seems.

Trample false perceptions
Birth forth with new conceptions
Refresh your inner thoughts
Recapture what you've sought.

How Vibrant Are We?

How vibrant are we
When we worship Thee
Our life has changed
Thoughts rearranged.

Free from despair
To now forbear.
Overcoming fear
Forgiving with cheer.

No redundancy
Filled with prophecy.
Inspirational motives
Rise up to focus.

One day at a time
Given to mankind.
Set forth belief
Ultimate relief!

The mercy seat
Kneel at His feet
How vibrant are we
When we worship Thee!

The Work Is Done

Holy Spirit come and bless my soul
Accept my thanks for making me whole
I long to have your voice to speak
Usher me to the highest peak!

When I am feeling all alone
I seek to hear from heaven's throne
Faith comes by the spoken word
The greatest message ever heard

Sometimes I stumble on my way
Get up child my Lord would say
He never scolded or put me down
He just planted me on solid ground.

Mistakes are made as yesterdays past
Forgiving oneself is the greatest task
I am lifted from any shame.
I give glory to His name.

I'm not so perfect, I have my scars
Thank you Lord for who you are
Merciful Father, all sufficient one
My Savior, my king, the work is done.

Treasures

Oh gallant rivers that rush and roar
Above it does the eagle soar.

I lift my eyes to capture the sight
As waves of beauty take its plight.

I tread upon the needled grain sand
Beholding the work of the Master's hand

I run in chase of the gentle breeze
Then fall at last upon my knees

My heart gave pant and then applause
Life gave moment to a thankful cause.

A release in time that filled my mind
The chant of praise within did chime.

I rested in the seat of awesome bliss
Of all God's pleasures we so often miss.

My ship had finally come to shore
Bringing the treasures of life to adore!

Today

Thank you Lord for last night's rest
Rising today with out past stress.
I trust you as I walk each day
Your word I'll read and obey.

I need you Lord to possess my soul
Thus keep the promises as foretold
I will not walk in selfishness
It only leads to slowed success.

Today I vow to lift you up
Bittersweet may be the cup
I know you'll let the bitter pass
Troubles are not made to last.

I thank you for your birth and mine
I found you when my life was blind
I understand there are many plans
On righteousness I choose to stand.

Together we meet what is ahead
Help me accept old things as dead
The two of us an awesome pair
Today I acknowledge you everywhere.

Power in His Hand

Church bells are ringing
Let our hearts rejoice in singing
Our Savior and precious king
Sent by God to cleanse and redeem.

We bless His most holy name
Praise God the Savior came
Oh shout throughout the land
There is power in his hand!

The best that we can give
Is how we actually live
Cast no sorrow bring the joy
Open your heart to the poor.

Raise your arms and spirit high
All He asks is that you try
Give the Lord your very best
It is your life He came to bless.

This is the gift that we embrace
Just to look upon His face
Angels trump the heavenly sound
The Savior's grace, the awesome crown.

Angelic Breeze

If I had wings to fly away
To look into His face today
His eyes to heal my inner hurt
To move above earthly turf.

Praise and honor to my king
To lift my voice to Him I sing
Ah in love, the angelic breeze
In honor, I fell to my knees.

My heart to Him, I am received
Tis all I hoped, and yet believed
I feel the presence of His arm
Away from toil and any harm.

Oh Lord my precious Savior dear
With Him I have a perfect seer
A mind filled with love
My thoughts are up above.

Twas here I long to ever be
In a vision procured by thee
Oceans of grace move my soul
Oh "River of Life" forever hold.

Ring Every Bell and Chime

An immaculate birth in story
He came in awesome glory
Some may not understand
The love God has for man.

Take courage in what is heard
There is power in the word
He is the absolute reason
We embrace every season!

Christ lives in every heart
It's the music each day to start
Lift your voice in cheer
Sound the trumpet in every ear.

It is our business as usual
There cannot be refusal
Proclaim the coronation
He is our salvation.

Spread the love around
Take gifts throughout the town
Ring every bell and chime
Prepare for harvest time.

Oh Holy Spirit

Oh Holy Spirit, my sustainer and dayspring
You have become my motivator in all things
Yes, a stabilizing vision of what is to be
It is the daily pattern cut plain to see.

I am calmed by your inner voice
I long to make the correct choice
I rise each day by your amazing grace
With good intentions, I dare not waste.

You are my rescuer and closest friend
I welcome your presence; I invite you in
You are my anchor in heart and soul
I am thankful to be called into the fold.

You are my provision, my Jehovah Jireh
I am filled with treasures, Abundant Provider
Thank you for your continued correction
I will ever seek your guided direction.

When I am weary and sometimes worn
Capture my mind, become a sounding horn
Alert me for the tomorrows ahead
Teach me through your daily bread.

Everlasting Father

He is omnipotent
The everlasting Father
I stand in awe of Him!

He is all knowing
Compassionate and true
I raise my hands in praise!

His love is immeasurable
His blessings are limitless
I kneel in His presence!

He is omnipresent
His grace is sufficient
I walk in His love!

God is always at work
He is always there
I behold His glory!

He is creator of all things
His greatness is manifested
I tell of His power!

He sent His son
The ambassador to the saints
I live in victory!

Priceless Love

Thou have held my hand in weakness
Thus delivered me from the grave
Thou have purchased me
I paid no price.

You bathed my soul
I am cleansed
I am pulled from the ground
You are my sanctuary.

Thou have soothed me with oil
Your gentleness has calmed me
In the whisper of the wind
You summoned me.

You saw what no one had seen
You repaired the broken wall
Your words have taught me
I am on a pinnacle.

I am not afraid
Purple and scarlet clothe me
You have raptured me
I am understood.

Sacrifice

The crowd amazed
Some shouted with praise

He chose the day
Garments tossed in the way

In humble submission
As one with permission

In Jerusalem He came
The cross was His aim

On a lowly beast
They called the least

The hosanna cry
He would soon die

Salvation

The passion of many tears
Rolled away the clack of jeers
His scars bought birthright
The sweat sparked insight.

The spear opened the wound
The earth shaken with gloom
The darkness anchored fear
Yet it opened every deaf ear.

Innocent of human sin
Bearing the burden of all men
He called a prayer in pause
Forgiveness was the cause.

The thorns upon His brow
The head in curtsey bow
The bones could not be broke
For prophecy surely spoke.

Death had made an end
Redemption scored a win
Resurrection closed the grave
Salvation freely paid.

Approaching Him

I will approach the Lord my God
With a meek and humble spirit
I will search for Him in the morning
He has become my dayspring.

I will call the Lord upon my bed
He will visit me there as I rest
I long for His presence to fill my soul
I will approach the Lord my God.

I will dream of His goodness
And the fellowship of His love
He will sustain me as I walk before Him
His promises have become my raiment.

I am shielded by His glory in battle
I run in the noonday by His mercy
His weapons are my defense
I stand in the judgment of the Almighty.

His power is the strength of my day
He is always there to guide me
The Lord is the beauty of my life
He has approached me and I am saved.

Victorious

The palms, the branches
Did not bring answers
The ride through the city
Did not bring pity.

No one could possibly see
The love He has for you and me
The road of life ushered deep despair
He walked the path, our sins to bear.

The sweat, the blood marked His toil
Anointing our heads with precious oil
All God's creature's great and small
Had to be redeemed from that awful fall.

Hands pierced with deep nail scars
The temple, the veil torn apart
Shout hosanna, the worthy praise
He arose in victory to satan's amaze.

So wave the palm branches
Our Christ is the answer
Conquering death, hell and the grave
Our lives He triumphantly saved.

Dayspring

Oh wonderful Savior, sustainer and dayspring
You have become my motivator in all things
My stabilizing vision of what is to be
A daily pattern cut plain to see.

I am calmed by your whispering inner voice
Thank you for helping me view the right choice
I arise each day by your marvelous amazing grace
Your intentions for me, I am cautious not to waste.

My rescuer and my closest friend
I welcome you to enter in
You are the anchor of my heart and soul
I am a member of your bountiful fold.

You are my provision, my Jehovah Jireh
Overcome by treasures, my abundant supplier
Led by your grace and guided correction
Seeking your favor and financial direction.

When feeling weary and sometimes worn
Capture my mind, become my sounding horn
Touch me when I have reached my limit
By your power, I shall stand as vehement.

Ministering

Today, as I came to the door of the church
In a nearby car, there was a woman and a child
Her head was buried in her hands
I could hear the cry of the baby as I drew near.

I heard in my spirit the words from Isaiah
Comfort ye, comfort ye my people
Relieve now the oppressed and set the captive free
I was filled with compassion for her sorrow.

I asked, "What may I do to help you"?
We were strangers yet she was of my loins
She is of a different culture, yet she is my seed
I embraced her bruises and loved her baby son.

She told of her misfortune, a neighborhood conflict
I gave her of my substance; my hands warmed her face
What is this substance? The immeasurable love of God.
I offered to help in many innumerable ways.

She led me to her home, a village to plant a seed
This was Ruth and Naomi with our kinsman Redeemer
Lord help me with the strangers, I leave in your care
This is the beginning of a mission, the capturing of souls.

Prayer

Praying is wholeheartedly talking to God
It is an overwhelming urgency of the heart
Taking the time to pour oil from my vessel
I am in the secret place of myself.

No human is listening; there is no applause
There is no standing ovation, for what is said
The multitude of words cease, I am mute
I am no longer blind; I see the vision now.

I am not deaf; I have become a listener
I am rich yet poor in spirit
When I have no clue, He is my answer
When I fall, I am cushioned in His safety.

When I am blemished, He cleanses me there
When I am empty, He fills my reservoir
He is there, when I am forsaken
I shall pause and give Him praise.

Prayer has become my intimate desire
A spiritual rapture in the sanctuary of my soul
It is where victory is magnified in praise
It becomes the forerunner to my worship.

Prayer is when I applaud His works
My private collection in thought
A transcending of the spirit
The master is at work in me.

Inspirations By Faith

I am in the safe place of His word
I am ushered to acknowledge forgiveness
I embrace the peaceful co-existence
When I honor the Lord in prayer.

Peace

The starry skies opened up
And swallowed me from myself
I was high into the heavens
My lips spoke not a word.

Mine eyes beheld no mystery
Only beauty arrayed in splendor
As quietness mingled with silence
A melody was peacefully heard.

I moved across the atmosphere
My feet did not motion to walk
No one noticed I was missing
My name seemed as unknown.

The clock never stopped movement
Time waited only for a moment
While I visited a place called peace
Then the mind returned back home.

Words

Let my words pomp for silence
Yet move the mountain of violence
Let my words always be plain
Removing any guilt or blame.

Let my words come with reason
And compliment on every season
Let my words come to search
Those that may enter in the church.

Let my words come with power
To refresh the earth this hour.
Let my words come to replenish
That the obstinate will relinquish.

Let my words give satisfaction
A charge to those in distraction
Let my words come not to confuse
To ridicule or accuse.

Let my words come to soothe
All heartache to remove
Let my words follow to calm
Providing an extended arm.

Let my words provide a peace
For God's love will never cease
Let my words provide a token
To every heart that's broken!

A Baby's Prayer

Dear Mommy, Daddy and Brother too
Your faith in God is ever true.

I stayed in Mommy for just a while
Then angels came to rapture her child.

I did not come to speak a word
Yet in silence I'm forever heard.

Thanks for all the precious things
God came and gave me angel's wings.

Now let me fly away and be
In heaven I will wait for thee.

In The Glimpse of a Day

In the night closest to morning
There is a quiet place
The heart awakens from sleep
Spirit and mind come together.

Thoughts begin to surface
Yesterday cannot be found
Failures are forgotten
There is a washing of the soul.

Stretch forth into focus
The new ideas of today
Reach out and touch progress
Let reality critique to time.

Movement maintains connection
Instinct runs in motion
Revival takes its place
In the glimpse of a day.

A Father's Hymn

The thunder of your storm
May shake you through the years
Painted rainbows may not last
Yet fatherhood stands the test of time.

Water may cloud your eyes
No matter how hard you try
Yet strength will applaud you
When weakness ushers by.

Past faults come to plague
Do not let them linger there
Create a circle from the good
Let nothing break your path.

Pain may walk your floor
Take heed to the excellent way
Your lips shall speak of praise
Your arms reach forth in love.

Live in balance by His power
Never fear the unknown
Stand tall oh father of tomorrow
Renew your strength, father today.

In the Joy of Life

Walk your path
Even when weary
Move with diligence
Let cause make effect.

Belief is crucial
Work is credible
Failure makes recovery
Vision meets progression.

Ideas are common
Orchestrate the dream
Truth builds character
Pulling takes force.

Listening develops wisdom
Planning is foremost
Light breaks darkness
Frustration lifts to challenge.

A seed is planted
Cultivate with understanding
Passion finds fulfillment
In the joy of a life.

Reaching

Do people really care?
Is there a cross to bear?
Clutching for good health
Wishing for life's wealth.

Show a smile upon the face
Relished by His loving embrace
Walk in delightful winds
When patience wears real thin.

Man's vision on the earth
Evolves on selfish worth
A focus on corporate means
The stamina that it brings.

The presence of His peace
Let's try to really reach
As strength forbears the weak
It crushes all defeat.

Burst Forth

The beauty of the race
Created with elegant taste
Like a perfect flower
Seeds bursting forth in power.

There are differential colors
Yet woven like no other
A multi-cultural language
Without a hint of anguish.

As love freely abides
Burst forth with human pride
Build a fence of peace
Pray struggles to release.

Now faces may even vary
Let the heart of each be merry
Now join the earthly chorus
Shout, for God is for us.

This Morning

This morning, I flew above the horizons
Beyond my situations and things that are
Higher than the birds and trees
Soaring as never before.

My breath was taken from me
Excitement filled my soul
Silenced by awe, I beheld the beauty
The wonder of all creative things.

Mercy and truth covered all that existed
I beheld the greatness of His power
A brightness that overcomes any darkness
I shouted a morning praise.

As I returned to the morning of life
Enlightened by faith in myself
Refreshed for today's journey
Armed for the enemy.

Compelled to be productive
Observant of simple things
Pulling off yesterday's garments
I embraced the joy of the morning.

Freedom

Freedom is an empowered place
A celebration of God's grace
Delegating decisions made
To walk and not be afraid.

Declaring basic rights
The relevance of human life
Walking the land without blame
The right to occupy free of shame.

To escape the burden of captivity's pain
Maintain a focus on educational aims
Released from the clutches of sin
Gracious for the victory to win.

Freedom is maintaining pride
Liberty that is expressed worldwide
The right to independent speech
To develop goals within one's reach.

The will to have a dream
To motivate self-esteem
The power to raise a nation
Maintain a standard of all creation.

Quiet Spirit

The quiet spirit prays within
Pondering the good and the bad
Thinking of past, present, and future
Having a revival within the soul.

The quiet spirit is gentle
Speaking to God in silence
Presenting the alms on the altar
Encouraging all that come.

It mingles in the sanctuary
Graciously considers others
Passionate about the kingdom plan
Tolerant of the misinformed.

The quiet spirit honors prudence
Speaks with calm awareness
Relates to sensitivity
Observes responsiveness.

It anchors in progression
Satisfied by endearing things
Prompted by excitement
Walks in righteousness.

It looks beyond the surface
Maintains the raging storm
Fulfills the daily tasks
Calms the roaring lion.

It's the witness for the ministry
Receiving grace from the Highest Power
Nourishes its own self-healing
The spirit of the Church.

The Night

Whose footsteps trample through the night?
When the sun is out of sight
Prowling under the heavy dark
Steps that never leave a mark.

Shadows cast upon the walk
There is no sound of talk
Leaves are stirring on the lawn
Trampled by the spotted pawn.

When the world seems to rest
Creatures roam in the crest
Flowers seem to fold in prayer
For every petal made with care.

When blackness pours upon the blue
As the night awaits the dew
All the beauty is quiet and still
The moon far above the hills.

Who is nesting in the trees?
As others fly above the seas
Creatures living great and tall
Responding to distinctive calls.

Clay

A beautiful collection
Clay shaped unto perfection
Sculptured in special design
Everyone is unique in kind.

The complexity of thought
The magnitude it brought
A development sure and grand
Not made by human hand.

The elegance of His Speech
Framed the earth beneath
Thus man is truly blessed
Yes, a gift of God's best.

There is an Awesome Power
As fragrant as the flower
That multiplies time and space
A beauty to embrace.

It's Me

I move through life with my sweetness
My tender way of entering the soul
I fly upon the wings of the heart
    It's me Love

Lurking in the shadows waiting
When a heart needs mending
Wiping the tear flowing eyes
    It's me Love

Chasing through fields locking hands
An interwoven spirit arm in arm
Coming together in unspoken words
    It's me Love

Releasing to the lost, a path
Gentleness to the belligerent
A trail for the unforgiving
    It's me, Love

The strength that binds
The adhesiveness of a nation
The bond and blood in creation
    It's me, Love

Oh chosen one of myself
Come and be mine
For I am forever yours
    It's me, your Love!

Cry Aloud

Cry aloud for the death on the street
Despite the victim you did not meet
Cry aloud for the outcast one
Under the bridge by the river run.

Cry aloud for the sin and shame
Bind every darkness in Jesus name
Cry aloud for every angry threat
For Jesus Christ has paid the debt.

Cry aloud where injustice hides
Build us Lord on sacred pride
Cry aloud for the morning after
Youth filled with temporal laughter.

Cry aloud for the instant fix
Packaged as the enemy's trick
Cry aloud for every generation
Power to combat deterioration.

Cry aloud for mass deception
The faithful Lord is our protection
Cry aloud for all the schools
Seat each principle by the golden rule.

Grandparents

They sit on thrones not so high
They enjoy just singing a lullaby
They take much pride in all they see
Saying, oh that child does favor me.

They preach, don't spank or raise your voice
Cautioning that children really deserve a choice
They close their lips and seal them ever so tight
When listening to secrets, they are out of sight.

Their pockets are always filled with coins
Fulfilling the mission to a child's open loins
They laugh and cheer to those on the street
Showing sweet photos to those they meet.

They pull the children out of the stall
They are off to loiter at the shopping mall
They volunteer to baby sit at their home
Then they refuse to answer the phone.

Dealing with homework is not their bag
This seems to make them stutter and gag.
The joys that grandparents bring to life
They are jewels of honor without a price.

A Love That Satisfies

I find in thee oh Lord
A love that satisfies
Weary heart and empty soul
You found me.

I am swelled by your power
You have inflated me
Your mercy is consuming
I rise with momentum.

You have coerced me
The spindle has refined me
I am developed
Completely comprehensible.

The petals of life break open
I release a new energy
I am inspired
Purpose becomes promise!

Building

I will build for you a special place
First within my heart and soul
This means that you have priority
For you are my very first love.

I promise to rise in the morning
And give you praise and worship
Building on every foundational impulse
You place within my spirit.

I cherish the flowers you gave me
That blossomed from your word
Encouraged to build the missions
That others may walk this path.

Thank you for whispering in my ear
The message of strength today
I'm building on that premise
This is the place I choose.

I found a safe haven in you
Protected by your shelter of love
My building is so content
I am happy in every room.

My hands are held by your comfort
Lord, you enabled me
I will build a monument of praise
For your faithful love to me.

Blessings

Thank you Lord for choosing me
To be a Mother, how I praise thee
You taught me how to give of myself
I cherish this gift, a pleasurable wealth.

Oh what joy to love a child!
To watch my angel bring forth a smile
A challenge for life, a given task
To do my best is all I ask.

The statues from your word I teach
Keeping your wisdom within my reach
I promise to mold and beautifully shape
Forgive me when I make mistakes.

Watching my child when at rest
Praying faithfully through every test
In thundering storms, to God be the glory
For you make life a worthwhile story.

Endless Love

It seems like only a yesterday
God led us in this pathway
Strangers yet we became friends
He showed us a love that had no end.

It was only a time ago
Our eyes were set, our hearts a glow
Excitement moved with every step
Hoping promises would always be kept.

It has been a many tomorrows
Hopes of love bringing no sorrow
Finding a place we only knew
Whether dawn, dusk or morning dew.

It is only in life's fulfillment
We look away in this contentment
Embracing the love of the moment
We cherish the God given proponent.

Beholding what is yet to come
Trusting where blessings are from
We hurt, forget, and work to forgive
In His love we will forever live.

These Two as One

He said, the flock would at first be small
She so eagerly sanctioned the divine call
He walked the innocence of this perfect way
She heard the thunder, saw clouds of gray.

The Fathers of old counseled him through
She prayed at the alter and sat in the pew
The ground was level and the pasture green
No fruitless orchards they would ever dream.

The impressionable vision will ever be bright
They never saw chance of a sleepless night
They held to God through every blissful hour
Knowing the mission was to obviously empower.

His loins are filled with gospel preaching
She prays that God would anoint his speaking
Hand in hand they feel the hearts of the people
Letting their spirits soar high as an eagle.

They chase away thoughts of giving up
Despite drinking the bitter sweet cup
They have learned to serve by example
Their blessings are sufficiently ample.

Mothers of Honor

Mothers are the fragrance of roses
They kneel to pray as God proposes
Finding a way to hide the tears
When life's sweet work brings on fears.

Mothers build a standard
Lighting the fire of a lantern
Guiding the footsteps on the way
Setting the pace throughout the day.

Who will come to make her smile?
Perhaps ease her tasks for a while
Patience and stamina is her glove
Mercy and truth meet from above.

Mothers bathe and care for fevers
Knowing that God is her reliever
Meditating on things that seem so small
A glimpse of momentum grand and tall.

Mothers may ponder and dare to speak
When in her bosom a crisis sleeps
Creeping to arise to cause some pain
Standing still is her battle in aim.

A Mother's face should always be kind
Rearing the children really takes time
Submitting good attitudes for the quest
Knowing that you have given your best.

Mothers have certainly paid the price
All the praise she gives to Christ
They are the warriors in this race
Let's honor their precious place.

The Light of Night

The candle of the night is burning
Thoughts of love are ever yearning
A memory of what brought me here
The calling voice rings so clear.

Who sought me on this narrow path?
Why do I really need to ask?
Oh sweet bright and shining star
Running in the distance far.

Never chase the night away
Come true fountain ever stay
Hold my hand and draw me near
Trample down the hidden fear.

All creation stands in awe
Abiding by your perfect law
Quench the thirst, feed my soul
Fill me now and make me whole.

I rest upon life's comfort chair
Knowing your love is always there
Strength is what I really seek
Let me rise to a higher peak.

As I walk just let me beam
Laughter burst me at the seam
The scars of old are trampled down
I shall not hear its weary sound.

With your love, I've done my best
Touch me gently as I rest
Pave the way for tomorrow's journey
The candle of night is ever burning.

Printed in the United States
106331LV00002B/355-372/A